Samuel French Acting Edition

Theater Masters' Take Ten Volume IV

First Contact
Liam Fitzgerald

The Death of Odysseus
or Pete and Jasper Need a Roommate
Liz Baker

The Moment After
Michael John McGoldrick

Pining
Banna Desta

Slap
Aja Nisenson

T3MPORARY
Joe Samaniego

SAMUELFRENCH.COM   SAMUELFRENCH.CO.UK

Introduction Copyright © 2019
First Contact © 2019 by Liam Fitzgerald
The Death of Odysseus © 2019 by Liz Baker
The Moment After © 2019 by Michael John McGoldrick
Pining © 2019 by Banna Desta
Slap © 2019 by Aja Nisenson
T3MP0RARY © 2019 by Joe Samaniego
All Rights Reserved

THEATER MASTERS' TAKE TEN, VOLUME IV is fully protected under the copyright laws of the United States of America, the British Commonwealth, including Canada, and all other countries of the Copyright Union. All rights, including professional and amateur stage productions, recitation, lecturing, public reading, motion picture, radio broadcasting, television and the rights of translation into foreign languages are strictly reserved.

ISBN 978-0-573-70775-9

www.SamuelFrench.com
www.SamuelFrench.co.uk

FOR PRODUCTION ENQUIRIES

UNITED STATES AND CANADA
Info@SamuelFrench.com
1-866-598-8449

UNITED KINGDOM AND EUROPE
Plays@SamuelFrench.co.uk
020-7255-4302

Each title is subject to availability from Samuel French, depending upon country of performance. Please be aware that *THEATER MASTERS' TAKE TEN, VOLUME IV* may not be licensed by Samuel French in your territory. Professional and amateur producers should contact the nearest Samuel French office or licensing partner to verify availability.

CAUTION: Professional and amateur producers are hereby warned that *THEATER MASTERS' TAKE TEN, VOLUME IV* is subject to a licensing fee. Publication of this play(s) does not imply availability for performance. Both amateurs and professionals considering a production are strongly advised to apply to Samuel French before starting rehearsals, advertising, or booking a theatre. A licensing fee must be paid whether the title(s) is presented for charity or gain and whether or not admission is charged. Professional/Stock licensing fees are quoted upon application to Samuel French.

No one shall make any changes in this title(s) for the purpose of production. No part of this book may be reproduced, stored in a retrieval system, or transmitted in any form, by any means, now known or yet to be invented, including mechanical, electronic, photocopying, recording, videotaping, or otherwise, without the prior written permission of the publisher. No one shall upload this title(s), or part of this title(s), to any social media websites.

For all enquiries regarding motion picture, television, and other media rights, please contact Samuel French.

MUSIC USE NOTE

Licensees are solely responsible for obtaining formal written permission from copyright owners to use copyrighted music in the performance of this play and are strongly cautioned to do so. If no such permission is obtained by the licensee, then the licensee must use only original music that the licensee owns and controls. Licensees are solely responsible and liable for all music clearances and shall indemnify the copyright owners of the play(s) and their licensing agent, Samuel French, against any costs, expenses, losses and liabilities arising from the use of music by licensees. Please contact the appropriate music licensing authority in your territory for the rights to any incidental music.

IMPORTANT BILLING AND CREDIT REQUIREMENTS

If you have obtained performance rights to this title, please refer to your licensing agreement for important billing and credit requirements.

THEATER MASTERS STAFF/BOARD

Daisy Walker, Executive Artistic Director
Victoria Hansen, Co-Artistic Director
Emily Zemba, Producing Director
Julia Hansen, Founder/Artistic Advisor

Advisory Board: Chris Ashley, Alec Baldwin, Andre Bishop, Gordon Davidson, Scott Ellis, A.R. Gurney, Doug Hughes, Judy Kaye, Andrew Leynse, John Lithgow, Robert Moss, Brian Murray, Jack O'Brien, Neil Pepe, John Rando, Theresa Rebeck, Tim Sanford

Board of Directors: Julia Hansen, Susan Buckley, Nancy Dunlap, John Hoffman, Gerri Karetsky, Marianne Lubar, Naomi McDougall Jones, Staman Ogilvie, Virginia Pearce, Jessica Salet, Nancy Stevens, Charlotte Tripplehorn, Danielle Chock, Tracy Forristall

THEATER MASTERS 2018 STAFF

Julia Hansen, Founding Artistic Director, now Emeritus
Joseph Ward, Executive Artistic Director
Emily Zemba, General Manager

TAKE TEN 2018 ASPEN PRODUCTION TEAM

Mark C. Hoffner, Production Stage Manager, Sound Designer
Brett Maughan, Technical Director, Scenic & Lighting Designer
David Auburn, 2018 National Adjudicator
Abbie Van Nostrand, 2018 Distinguished Guest

TAKE TEN 2018 NEW YORK PRODUCTION TEAM

Judy Bowman, CSA, Casting
Mike Best, Technical Director/Properties Designer
Mark C. Hoffner, Sound Designer
Ben Kahre, Fight Director
Kevin Novinsky, Sound Consultant/Programmer
Driscoll Otto, Lighting & Projection Designer
Deidre Works, Production Stage Manager

INTRODUCTION

Julia Hansen founded the National MFA Playwrights Competition and Take Ten Festival in 2007 when she saw a need for an organization to bridge the gap between the academic training playwrights were receiving and the professional careers that lay ahead of them. Take Ten's dual professional development opportunity and this partnership with Samuel French provide playwrights with a career-igniting entrance into the entertainment industry and introduce their work to the American Theater.

Each year we invite MFA playwrights from some of the top programs in the country to submit a ten-minute play. The six to ten winning playwrights are flown to Aspen, Colorado for workshop productions with prominent directors and the local community of dedicated actors. In the spring, the playwrights and their directors travel to New York for an equity showcase production of their plays. Take Ten launches these young playwrights into the industry and provides a platform from which to share their unique voices in American Theater.

We are grateful to all who have supported our 2018 National MFA Playwrights Festival: the MFA programs across the country, including Arizona State University, Brown, Carnegie Mellon, Columbia, Fordham/Primary Stages, Northwestern, NYU, University of Iowa, University of Texas at Austin, UCLA, UCSD, and the Yale School of Drama, who recognize talented students; our professional directors who share their time, expertise, and vision – providing invaluable mentoring to their proteges; and finally our generous individual donors and board who make Take Ten possible.

We are passionate about these playwrights, and we hope you will enjoy this fourth anthology of Theater Masters' plays.

Sincerely,

Daisy Walker, Executive Artistic Director
Vicky Hansen, Co-Artistic Director

TABLE OF CONTENTS

First Contact 9
The Death of Odysseus 23
The Moment After 37
Pining 47
Slap 59
T3MP0RARY 73

First Contact

Liam Fitzgerald

FIRST CONTACT was first produced by Theater Masters in Aspen, Colorado from February 11–13, 2018. The performance was directed by Joanie Schultz, and the production stage manager was Mark C. Hoffner. The cast was as follows:

JIMMY.. Haver Muss-Nichols
DANNY.. Talulah Marolt

FIRST CONTACT was first produced by Theater Masters and Rattlestick Playwrights Theater in New York City from May 1–5, 2018. The performance was directed by Joanie Schultz, and the production stage manager was Deidre Works. The cast was as follows:

JIMMY.. Eli Tokash
DANNY... Alexa Shae Niziak

CHARACTERS

JIMMY – (13, male) The nerdiest nerd that ever nerded.
DANNY – (13, female) The second-nerdiest nerd that ever nerded.

SETTING

Clearing in the woods. This is their normal "search spot."

TIME

Late nineties to early 2000s.

AUTHOR'S NOTES

The characters talk fast and think mid-sentence. Everything should overlap unless otherwise specified. There are more throwaway lines than dramatic pauses.

"Beat" should be treated as a line of silence owned by a character.

A dash (–) indicates an interruption.

An ellipsis (...) indicates a trailing off.

(*JIMMY looks into a telescope. Around him are star charts and alien books. An "I want to believe" sticker is on his telescope. His bike is nearby, dropped to the ground.*)

(*He pulls out a walkie-talkie.*)

JIMMY. Hey. Are you coming? Over.

DANNY. *(Over walkie.)* Yeah. I'm on my way. Over.

JIMMY. How far are you? Over.

DANNY. *(Over walkie.)* Not far. Over.

JIMMY. How far is not far? Over.

DANNY. *(Over walkie.)* Really? Over.

JIMMY. Rough guess? Over.

DANNY. *(Over walkie.)* A lot faster if you stop radioing me.

(*Beat.*)

JIMMY.	**DANNY.**
You didn't say –	*(Over walkie.)* Over.

(*JIMMY paces for a moment, rehearsing something in his head.*)

(*DANNY enters on her bike. She throws it down next to Jimmy's.*)

DANNY. Heyo!

JIMMY. Oh, hi.

DANNY. Hi.

JIMMY. Hi.

DANNY. You said that.

JIMMY. What?

DANNY. Hi. You already said –

JIMMY. Oh. Yeah. Well... Hi.

DANNY. Dork. Sorry I'm late. My mom and dad were fighting. You start without me?

(She pulls out a well-worn notebook.)

JIMMY. Oh, yeah.

DANNY. Rude.

JIMMY. I just have to be back home by –

DANNY. I'm kidding. You're jumpy –

JIMMY. What?

DANNY. Jumpy. You're jumpy tonight.

JIMMY. Oh, yeah. I, guess. Yeah.

DANNY. You find any aliens yet?

JIMMY. Nope.

DANNY. What have you covered?

JIMMY. Sector sixty-four and sixty-five.

DANNY. Got it. Sixty-four and sixty-five, nothing.

JIMMY. Well, no.

It's not nothing.

JIMMY.	**DANNY.**
Not really. There are thousands of stars and other…so to say nothing is really not accurate.	I know that. I was just… Fine.

DANNY. Sectors sixty-four and sixty-five, no aliens.

JIMMY. And we don't really know if –

DANNY. No "totally obvious" aliens.

JIMMY. I was just…words mean things.

JIMMY.	**DANNY.**
If we use them in the improper way they lose their meaning.	No, totally, that's totally… worth pointing out. Thank you, Jimmy.

*(Beat. **JIMMY** looks into the telescope.)*

JIMMY. I was doing that thing where I overexplain things in a jerky way –

DANNY. Yep.

(A light flashes across the stage.)

Look over there, there's a shooting star.

JIMMY. That's not...

DANNY. What is it?

JIMMY. I don't know.

> (**JIMMY** *swings his telescope to look.*)

DANNY. There's another one.

JIMMY. It's a shooting star.

DANNY. Told ya.

> (**DANNY** *records the sighting.* **JIMMY** *watches her for a while.*)
>
> (**DANNY** *pulls out her walkie.*)

(Into walkie.) Hey Jimmy. Why are you staring at me? Over.

JIMMY. I'm not staring –

DANNY.	**JIMMY.**
(Into walkie.) You're staring at me and you're super sweaty and it's kinda creepy.	It's hot I'm...

JIMMY. I'm not creepy! I was just looking over at the notes.

DANNY. *(Into walkie.)* I know when you're lying. Over.

JIMMY. No you don't.

DANNY.	
(Into walkie.) Uh-huh.	**JIMMY.**
Over.	Nuh-uh.

DANNY. *(Into walkie.)* Even the aliens secretly watching us know you're lying –

JIMMY. No, it's nothing. I'm not –

DANNY. *(Into walkie.)* Seriously dude. What is up? Over.

> (*Beat.* **JIMMY** *picks up his walkie.*)

JIMMY. *(Into walkie.)* I'm... I heard a rumor. Over.

DANNY. *(Into walkie.)* About what?

JIMMY. *(Into walkie.)* About you. Over.

DANNY. *(Into walkie.)* Okay. What are people saying about me? They saying I'm a nerd? That I'm not cool? Was it the hunting for aliens or was it –

JIMMY. *(Into walkie.)* It was about you and Derek. They said –

    (**DANNY** *puts the walkie down.*)

DANNY. Wait, what? What did uh... What did they say about us?

DANNY.	**JIMMY.**
Did they say anything about –	It's not, they uhm, they said you made out with him.

DANNY. Oh. Okay.

    (Beat.)

JIMMY. And that you gave him a hand job.

DANNY. God frickin' dammit. Frickin'...

DANNY.	**JIMMY.**
Frickin'. Fuck! That...shit burger. That fucking shit burger. Why would you do that, why would –	And I told them I didn't believe it for a second, I told them that you would never do that –

JIMMY. I told them he was lying. That you would never –

DANNY. Why? Why would you say that?

JIMMY. What?

DANNY. Why would you say I would never give Derek a hand job?

JIMMY. Why would I... 'Cause you wouldn't... 'Cause it's a rumor...right?

    (Beat.)

DANNY. Uhm. Yeah, I guess. I guess, yeah. Thanks for... straightening that out.

JIMMY. Of course... 'Cause like Derek right? Like that would be... I mean he's...totally gross.

DANNY. I wouldn't say gross.
JIMMY. No, he is totally –
DANNY. He's really not that –
JIMMY. He's a gross jerk.
DANNY. You'd like him. If you –
JIMMY. No I wouldn't. We have nothing in common.
DANNY. I think you might. I think you might...get along.

(*A long beat.*)

'Cause. If... Hypothetically, if I like, had –
JIMMY. We should...get back to the...sky. Sector sixty-six is...
DANNY. We already did sector sixty-six.
JIMMY. Okay, sector sixty-seven then.
DANNY. Okay. Right.

(*Beat.*)

This is why I didn't want you to know.
JIMMY. About the rumor?
DANNY. Yeah. The rumor.
JIMMY. Why would...like, there's nothing...nothing like, nothing for me to be...you know, like and even if it was. There isn't any reason...you know, why, why, why would –

(*He fake laughs.*)

Why, would I...care? What would I...you know?
DANNY. I guess you don't have a reason to.
JIMMY. Right. So. So. Right. Right. Cool. Cool cool. Yeah.

(**JIMMY** *goes back to the telescope.*)

Sector six...uhm sector sixty-seven...is clear.
DANNY. Sixty-seven. Nothing. Or, no obvious...yeah.

(*Beat.*)

I just want to say. If I heard that you had made out with someone.
Even if it was someone who, like, I didn't like –

JIMMY. Who would I make out with?

DANNY. Alice.

JIMMY. Alice would never make out with me.

DANNY. If she did.

JIMMY. She wouldn't.

DANNY. If she –

JIMMY. But –

DANNY. IF SHE DID.

I would be happy for you. I would congratulate you. As your friend, I would –

JIMMY.

But she just wouldn't make out with me, so I'm not sure what you're –

DANNY.
Jimmy, you're missing the –

JIMMY. Plus, like Alice, is, you can't compare Alice and Derek. Derek is a total jerk, nobody wants to make out with Derek.

DANNY. According to you.

JIMMY. According to...logic.

DANNY. Well... I like Derek. I don't think he's a jerk.

JIMMY. You don't like Derek.

DANNY. Yes I do.

(Beat.)

JIMMY. You don't spend any time with him. If you liked him, you'd, you'd spend time with him.

DANNY. I guess I don't, or didn't, but like, I like him now. Like I like-like him.

Or at least I did before he told everyone.

JIMMY. That's...that doesn't, people should like...people should like-like who they like. Like they should like-like people they spend time with and have fun with and they should make out and...you know with those people. Because that...those people make sense you know? Like I wouldn't make out with Alice because I don't like her. I don't spend time with her. She wouldn't make sense for me to –

DANNY. You would totally make out with Alice.

JIMMY. No I wouldn't and –

DANNY. Yes you would.

JIMMY. That's not the point.

DANNY. You're saying if Alice Thomson came up to you and said, "Jimmy let me make out with you. Pull out your donger and I'll –"

JIMMY.	**DANNY.**
Alice Thomson would never say donger.	You would say no?
And even if –	I'm sure she would if –

JIMMY. Fine. I would. I would make out with Alice and... yes. If she asked. I guess. I mean...yeah. Yeah, I would. Okay?

(Beat.)

DANNY. Well I made out with Derek.

(Beat.)

JIMMY. Why didn't you tell me?

DANNY. I didn't want to hurt you.

DANNY.	**JIMMY.**
I didn't want to ruin our friendship.	Why would that hurt me?

JIMMY. Why would that hurt me? Why would that ruin –

DANNY. I didn't want you to...you know...be upset.

JIMMY. Why would I be upset?

DANNY. You are. You are upset. I told you and you're upset.

(Beat.)

JIMMY. I'm not.

DANNY. Jimmy –

JIMMY. I'm not like upset about you, like you can...like why would I, why would I be upset about that? You know?

I'm just confused. I'm confused because Derek doesn't make sense, you know? With you. He's just weird with you. You and him don't make sense. He does sports and...it's not like he's popular it's... It's just weird. You two don't fit. You should...be with someone who makes sense.

DANNY. Like you?

JIMMY. I, uh...no not necessarily. But that would make sense. Right? Like...

(Beat. **JIMMY** *returns to his telescope.)*

JIMMY.	**DANNY.**
Sector sixty-eight has a lot of...there's a meteor shower or something.	Jimmy...

JIMMY. Or...or it's just searchlights from the video store. Shoot. I...uh. I got excited there...for a moment.

(Beat.)

DANNY. You know what else doesn't make sense? Coming out at night looking for aliens.

JIMMY. Yeah, no one has ever told me that before. What are you my parents?

DANNY. You look up every night and you see nothing, but you still come out here.

You don't get mad at the sky 'cause it's...it's not showing you what you want, but...you...like it disappoints you, but you come out here anyway. 'Cause, like, I mean finding an alien would be great, but...like coming out here and watching the sky... That's pretty cool too. The sky, as-is, is pretty great.

(Beat.)

JIMMY. You come out here too.

DANNY. I don't really care about the sky or the aliens. I come to spend time with my best friend.

(Beat.)

JIMMY. Why not me?

DANNY. Did you want it to be –

JIMMY. I don't...yeah? Yeah. Or... I just figured...like it would...happen that way. You know?

DANNY. Well... It didn't... It didn't happen like that I guess. And, I mean, Derek has a brand-new Huffy, not some generic Target-brand bike, so that's pretty sweet.

JIMMY. I can get a –

DANNY. I'm Kidding. I'm Kidding.
I don't know why I...why it's, it's just...that's the way it happened, and I would say I'm sorry, but... I'm not. 'Cause, like I made out with a boy and it was really nice and –

JIMMY. I'm happy for you. I am. Congrats.

DANNY. Thank you.

> *(Beat.)*

JIMMY. Okay. Well...what do we do now?

> *(Beat. **DANNY** crosses to the telescope. She looks through the lens.)*

DANNY. I don't want to jinx it, but sector sixty-nine looks full of aliens. Also...sixty-nine so... Nice!

> *(She holds her hand up for a high five. **JIMMY** stands there for a moment before laughing and high-fiving her back. They return to their alien-hunting positions.)*

JIMMY. Derek is a jerk though.

DANNY. So are you. That's why you'll get along.

JIMMY. Sixty-nine is clear.

DANNY. Sixty-nine. No obvious aliens.

> *(Fade to black.)*

The Death of Odysseus
or Pete and Jasper Need a Roommate

Liz Baker

THE DEATH OF ODYSSEUS was first produced by Theater Masters in Aspen, Colorado from February 11–13, 2018. The performance was directed by Wes Grantom, and the production stage manager was Mark C. Hoffner. The cast was as follows:

PETE .... Brandon Joseph
JASPER .... Gerald Delisser

THE DEATH OF ODYSSEUS was first produced by Theater Masters and Rattlestick Playwrights Theater in New York City from May 1–5, 2018. The performance was directed by Wes Grantom, and the production stage manager was Deidre Works. The cast was as follows:

PETE .... Grant Harrison
JASPER .... Ryan George

CHARACTERS

PETE – (mid-twenties, male) Jasper's roommate
JASPER – (mid-twenties, male) Pete's roommate

SETTING

The steps outside of Pete and Jasper's apartment

TIME

The Present

AUTHOR'S NOTES

An ellipsis (...) indicates a trailing off.

A dash (–) indicates an interruption or short stop.

A slash (/) indicates the point of interruption when one character speaks over another.

(Front steps of a split-level. **PETE** *and* **JASPER** *stagger in, each carrying multiple grocery bags however they can – in elbow crooks, on individual fingers.)*

PETE. I just think it's the best game in – in – in – the WORLD, history, whatever of video games! Like I would pay any amount of money for *The Witcher* –!

JASPER. Sure, but eventually you realize it's doing the same basic shit that all games do! They send you out to accomplish a specific task, you do it, then rinse / and repeat!

PETE. It's the hero's journey!

JASPER. That's not – Hey, hey, dude wait!

*(***JASPER*** *drops his bags and kneels to peer at something on the ground.)*

PETE. Jasper, what are you doing?

JASPER. There's a bee. Hey, little buddy.

PETE. What the hell? Leave it alone!

JASPER. No, he needs help! He looks weak...

PETE. That thing's going to fly up into your face, sting you in the eyeball! Smush it!

JASPER. *(Suddenly serious.)* Pete. No. Bees are our friends.

*(***JASPER*** *rises and heads into the house.)*

PETE. Dude, what about the groceries?

(To the bee.) Don't you try anything. I'm just taking my food in, okay?

(He makes it into the house just as **JASPER** *returns with a bottle of water.)*

JASPER. *(To the bee.)* Now I know there's something else that's helpful... Sugar, I think. But here's some water for now. Hopefully you're just thirsty.

(He pours a sip of water inside the bottle cap and sets it down.)

*(**PETE** returns to grab Jasper's share of the groceries.)*

PETE. What happened to "one trip or die," man? We're up two flights of stairs and you abandoned us on level zero!

JASPER. Yes, but it was for a cause far greater than you or I. The life of a bee.

PETE. A bee.

JASPER. Yes! Think about it. What did we just buy at the store? Blueberries, strawberries, cherries. Greek yogurt. Your morning breakfast staples. Vital. What else?

PETE. I'm not going to recite the whole grocery list just so you can / prove some point.

JASPER. Peaches, apples, tomatoes. Canola oil. Celery, pears, plums – you're even wearing a cotton t-shirt! And that's just the stuff off the top of my head!

PETE. Back up. How does Greek yogurt factor in?

JASPER. Alfalfa owes its reproduction to bees. Cows eat alfalfa and produce milk and the Greeks have figured out how to make milk into yogurt that is even creamier and more / delicious than –!

PETE. Okay, okay! Got it. Bees are important.

JASPER. Uh-huh.

Hey, when you go back, would you mind grabbing some sugar? Little guy needs electrolytes.

PETE. For the love of God, Jasper –

JASPER. This is what it says to do online when you see a tired bee! Some parts sugar, some parts water, I don't remember exactly...

PETE. Have you looked this up before? On the odd chance that you'd encounter a tired bee?

JASPER. I went down a bit of a rabbit hole on the internet last night. It's just lucky that today's the day I find Odysseus here.

PETE. You named it?!

JASPER. He's a shrewd warrior king who we're going to get home.

PETE. I thought bees had a queen.

JASPER. Right. Penelope. I bet she's worried about him...

PETE. Oh my god.

JASPER. C'mon, Pete! Come on...

> *(Kissy face.)*

Gimme a lil sugar.

PETE. I'm going! Just – quit with the nonsense, alright?

> *(He exits.)*

JASPER. Oh, him? Don't you worry about Pete, Odysseus. He's got a mild case of stick-up-the-ass, but he's a good guy.
You're looking a little more lively after that drink. But not ready to fly yet, huh? Don't worry, we'll get ya there.

> *(**PETE** returns with a bag of sugar and a spoon.)*

Thanks. Now I think it's one part to two, sugar to water. No. Wait...water to sugar...

PETE. It's one tablespoon of sugar with two tablespoons of water. I looked it up.

JASPER. Aw yeah, my man Pete! Okay. Did you bring a dish or something?

PETE. Oh. No, I didn't think of that.

JASPER. It's cool.

> *(He uses his cupped hand to mix the sugar and water.)*

So...
Was it a relief to be able to walk across the living room without being crabbed at?

PETE. Heh. Yeah, I'm still not used to it. I'll tiptoe for the first few steps before I realize he's not there and I can walk like a normal human being.

JASPER. *(Imitating someone.)* Not a human being! A FREAKIN' ELEPHANT!

PETE. Ha! That's a pretty good impression.

JASPER. Poor Johnny boy. He was so very very stressed.

PETE. Is. Can't imagine anything's gonna get better with him now that he's moved in with…what was her name again?

JASPER. Melanie?

PETE. Melissa! Who also happens to be so very very stressed.

JASPER. They're meant to be.

PETE. I mean, he is planning on proposing to her so… hopefully they are.

JASPER. Is he now? And how'd you get this juicy bit of gossip?

PETE. Oh, you know him. It was like pulling teeth. But I saw the ring and there's not really a different conclusion to make so…he just wound up telling me.

JASPER. Huh. Well, good for them.

PETE. Good for us really. We can use our living room now.

JASPER. And generally live in our apartment like people and not silent movie characters.

PETE. Ha, yeah.

JASPER. It's just you and me now, buddy. Together forever.

PETE. *(Uncomfortable.)* Dude, c'mon.

JASPER. Alright.

(To Odysseus.) Here ya go, buddy. Climb on up.

(He puts his hand down for the bee to climb into.)

PETE. Woah, is he…? Dude, you're like the bee whisperer.

JASPER. Yeah, it's pretty cool.

Being genuine for just a second here… I'm honestly relieved. That John ended up being the one to move out and not you. I like living with you.

PETE. *(Uncomfortable.)* Yeah? Why's that?

JASPER. *(To Odysseus.)* I'm going to put you down now, buddy.

(To **PETE**.*)* I just think we have a good vibe. Our schedules more or less match up. We both like *Game of Thrones* and *The Witcher* –

PETE. Yeah, but you're defecting on *The Witcher* now.

JASPER. I just recognize that it has its limits entertainment-wise. I still like the game.

(Back to his point.) You're a good cook, I don't mind doing the dishes. You brought the Xbox, I brought the / TV –

PETE. Yeah yeah yeah yeah, man. We're good roommates. A match made in Craigslist heaven.

JASPER. *(Mischievous.)* I'm making you uncomfortable. Can't take a little emotional vulnerability, Petey boy?

PETE. You're being ridiculous. Why hasn't this thing taken off yet?

JASPER. Give him time! He's resting.

(Beat.)

PETE. We are going to have to find a new roommate now though.

JASPER. I know. Should we throw it to Craigslist...? Or did you have someone in mind?

PETE. Um... Nah, that wouldn't work.

JASPER. Who?

PETE. I have a friend moving to town, but she's...an ex. Probably be awkward.

JASPER. Huh. You think?

PETE. I don't wanna live with her. She's not – she's not very clean. She sleeps in until like two in the afternoon. Wouldn't be the right fit.

JASPER. Hey, if you don't want to...

PETE. I don't wanna look for a third roommate at all, but we have to.

JASPER. Yeah.

PETE. How's our little buddy doing?

JASPER. "Our buddy"? Are you getting attached?

PETE. No. Maybe. You're the one who named him.

JASPER. Yeah, I shouldn't've done that.
(*To Odysseus.*) I'm very invested in your recovery now, little guy. And not just because your species determines the survival of my species. So...y'know, no pressure!

PETE. I'm...impressed. You seriously did your research.

JASPER. Like I said, I got very sucked into procrastination reading last night. Besides, bees are super interesting. Apparently they're what ecologists call an "indicator species."

PETE. Indicator...indicating what exactly?

JASPER. Only our impending doom. You know how coal miners would take canaries with them into the mines? And if the canary died, that was the sign to get the hell outta there. Bees are that, but for the world. Like, if environmental factors are killing bees off, then the situation is getting to the point where humans won't survive either.

PETE. Woah.

JASPER. Yeah, it's intense. And they're dying off in huge amounts so humans are totally doomed. Everything is, really...

PETE. Huh. That's funny.

JASPER. What?

PETE. You just reminded me of this song. Last night, while you were on your way to becoming a bee expert –

JASPER. Apiarist. Go on.

PETE. Right. I was – ya know those moods where you just listen to one song over and over and over again? Anyway, I've been listening to a lot of Father John Misty lately and...

JASPER. Father John Misty. Great band name.

PETE. You've never heard of Father John Misty?! Dude, you'd love him! He's got this whole indie-folk-nihilist-electronic vibe going on. He's awesome.

JASPER. What was the name of the song?

PETE. *(A bit embarrassed.)* "I Love You, Honeybear."

JASPER. Okay. And what reminded you...?

PETE. Well, there's this one line. Actually it's kinda the whole thing. Here, lemme...

> *(He pulls out a pair of earbuds and plugs them into his phone. He scoots closer to **JASPER** so they can share.)*
>
> *(Once they're connected, **PETE** presses play.*)*

Okay, so first it's like this Old-West piano and then...

> *(He half hums, half bops his head to the music. **JASPER** watches him out of the corner of his eye.)*

JASPER. Very nihilistic, yeah.

PETE. And poetic, right? Wait, wait, here's the part...it gets quiet and then...

JASPER. I love you.

PETE. Yeah. Yeah, that's the line and then it goes...

> *(Realizing.)*

Oh.

> *(**JASPER** leans in. A half-beat of hesitation, then **PETE** follows suit.)*
>
> *(They kiss. With enthusiasm.)*
>
> *(Off in the distance, a screech of brakes and several car horns. The spell is broken.)*

JASPER. *(In the direction of the cars.)* Woah. That was an asshole move, buddy.

PETE. Um?! Wh-what just happened?!

JASPER. Well, that Prius just tried to squeeze through a yellow and the truck –

PETE. Not that!

A-are you even gay, man?!

---

*The audience does not hear the song.

JASPER. That's not how I would put it.

PETE. I've just never seen you dating anyone and I never thought to ask –!

JASPER. Listen, Pete, I'm open to whatever happens to cross my path. Women, men, genderqueer... But I don't think that's what your problem is.

C'mon. Sit down, man. Your brain's gonna short out.

(Down at Odysseus.) Oh. Oh, man. You still with us, buddy?

PETE. Huh?

JASPER. I think Odysseus is... Yeah. He's dead.

(Beat.)

PETE. What...do we do?

JASPER. About which thing? Listen, we can just put this on the back burner for the moment. You don't need to slap a label on your sexuality / right away.

PETE. No, I meant Odysseus. We can't just leave him on the steps like this. He'll get smushed.

JASPER. Oh. I dunno. We could bury him in that little garden plot in the backyard.

PETE. But he's *Odysseus*. I feel like we should bury him at sea. Send him off in a little origami boat. Light it on fire. A whole Greek warrior funeral.

JASPER. That's Vikings, not the Greeks.

Nah, man. He served the earth in life, he shall serve the earth in death. Become fertilizer for our garden.

PETE. We don't have a garden.

JASPER. So we'll plant one! With flowers. Stuff that bees like. There's a list online.

PETE. We could make plaques. "In Loving Memory of Odysseus the Bee."

JASPER. C'mon, man. Don't be like that.

PETE. No, I'm serious. It's a good idea, Jasper.

JASPER. Yeah?

PETE. Yeah. Where would we get that stuff? Hardware store? They have seeds there, right?

 (He kneels down and scoops up Odysseus.)

JASPER. Yeah, Home Depot or somewhere.
Thanks, man.

PETE. No problem, buddy.

 (They exit.)

The Moment After

Michael John McGoldrick

THE MOMENT AFTER was first produced by Theater Masters in Aspen, Colorado from February 11–13, 2018. The performance was directed by Wes Grantom, and the production stage manager was Mark C. Hoffner. The cast was as follows:

KATIE .... Sonia Meyer
RYAN. .... Brendan T. Cochran

THE MOMENT AFTER was first produced by Theater Masters and Rattlestick Playwrights Theater in New York City from May 1–5, 2018. The performance was directed by Wes Grantom, and the production stage manager was Deidre Works. The cast was as follows:

KATIE .... Mikaela Izquierdo
RYAN. .... Ryan George

CHARACTERS

KATIE – female, late twenties
RYAN – male, late twenties

SETTING

An undefined space

TIME

The Present

(A bare stage. **KATIE** *and* **RYAN**, *in separate realities. Both speak directly to the audience.)*

KATIE. Love.

RYAN. Love.

KATIE. I used to believe in it.

RYAN. Never believed in it.

KATIE. One person for the rest of your life.

RYAN. Dopamine. Chemicals in the brain.

KATIE. For better or worse.

RYAN. That's love for you.

KATIE. Someone to understand you –

RYAN. They're nice chemicals.

KATIE. – the deepest part of you –

RYAN. But they're still chemicals.

KATIE. – and that's why I got married.

RYAN. Never married.

KATIE. Because I wanted that.

RYAN. Never with someone more than a year.

KATIE. I thought I had that. With Paul.

RYAN. 'Cause why bother? Chemicals don't stick around.

KATIE. I thought he really loved me.

RYAN. One time, I thought *maybe*.

KATIE. And when it started going wrong –

RYAN. With Marla. But no.

KATIE. – I fought to make it right.

RYAN. I wanted it. But it still fell apart.

KATIE. But he wasn't happy.

RYAN. So what's that prove?

KATIE. We weren't happy.

RYAN. Chemicals, man. When they're gone, I'm gone.

KATIE. I think a lot of it had to do with sex.

RYAN. Sex.

KATIE. Sex.

RYAN. More chemicals.

KATIE. I've always been sexually inhibited, okay?

RYAN. More chemicals than a relationship. So who needs the relationship?

KATIE. I'm not gonna tell you why. Okay, it's religion. But I'm not gonna get into that.

RYAN. And I'll tell you something else. It ain't politically correct or whatever, but what the fuck.

KATIE. Paul was the same way. Inhibited.

RYAN. When you're with a woman, everything depends on what happens in the bedroom.

KATIE. So our sex wasn't...good.

RYAN. Make her happy there, you're golden.

KATIE. We both tried. But no.

RYAN. Get her off on a regular basis and she'll put up with a lot of shit.

KATIE. And I kept at it. Trying to make him happy. 'Cause I thought I was supposed to.

RYAN. And I get the job done. That's not bragging. Just a fact.

KATIE. So when he said he was leaving – it was like a slap in the face.

RYAN. And the women I'm with – do I give them a lot of shit? Yeah, you got me there.

KATIE. I'm like, "What have I been doing all this time?"

RYAN. I feel a little guilty about that.

KATIE. "I've been offering myself to you!" You know what? I can't talk about this.

RYAN. It was different with Marla. I was good to her.

KATIE. I was hurt. And mad. That's all I can say about it.

RYAN. But it still fell apart. I don't like to think about that.

KATIE. So I decided to do something.

RYAN. Better not to think. Just do.

KATIE. Just do.

KATIE & RYAN. So I was at this bar.

KATIE. I didn't know what I was gonna do that night. Okay, I *knew*, but I *didn't* know, if you know what I mean.

RYAN. Just there on a Saturday. To see what I could see.

KATIE. I saw this guy and had him pegged.

RYAN. I saw this girl and had her pegged.

KATIE & RYAN. Wants to get laid.

(Beat.)

And I'm like, "Okay."

KATIE. I thought, why not? Don't I deserve this?

RYAN. She was cute in a mousy sort of way.

KATIE. And he was gorgeous.

RYAN. Not really my type. But it was getting late.

KATIE. And I was drunk. So the inhibitions were less.

KATIE & RYAN. I figured I'd go with it.

KATIE. So we're back at his place.

RYAN. And I'm warming her up.

KATIE. And we're making out.

RYAN. And then we're at it.

KATIE & RYAN. And suddenly –

KATIE. – something comes over me.

RYAN. – she's different.

KATIE. I like became a different person.

RYAN. Can't even describe it.

KATIE. It was me, but *not* me. Does that make sense?

RYAN. I'm doing my thing. But now she's *with it* in a way that's different.

KATIE. I'm totally present. But I'm like *performing*.

RYAN. And me. I got this method, okay? It's not an act, but yeah, it kind of is.

KATIE. I'm doing what I do with Paul.

RYAN. I just know what to do.

KATIE. But I'm like, "I'm gonna do a perfect version of that." As an act.

RYAN. But, like, I'm conscious of it? Does that make sense?

KATIE. But the *effort* it took with Paul. That's gone.

RYAN. But suddenly, I'm not conscious anymore. It's just *happening*.

KATIE. And right when we're really at it –

RYAN. And right when we're really at it –

KATIE. – the act slips away –

RYAN. – the act slips away –

KATIE. – and it's –

KATIE & RYAN. – *unbelievably real.*

    (Pause.)

KATIE. But after.

RYAN. After.

KATIE. I get weird.

RYAN. She's all different again.

KATIE. I don't know what this means.

RYAN. Something's up and I can't figure it.

KATIE. Because I'm me again. Like, day-to-day me.

RYAN. And I want her to stay, which is weird for me –

KATIE. I don't feel like the person who did that. So I gotta go.

RYAN. – and now she's up –

KATIE. I'm putting on my clothes –

RYAN. – and I'm watching her –

KATIE. – and he's watching me –

RYAN. – and the streetlight comes through the window and falls on her body –

KATIE. – and I feel weird weird weird and I'm thinking, "What do I say?" –

RYAN. – and she turns to me –

KATIE. – and I turn to him –

RYAN.	**KATIE.**
– and she gives me this look.	– and he gives me this look.
(Beat.)	*(Beat.)*
I can't even describe it.	I can't even describe it.
(Pause.)	

RYAN. I think it was confusion.

KATIE. I think it was pain.

RYAN. Like she was in some kind of pain and didn't know why.

KATIE. Like he was confused by what he was feeling and didn't know why.

KATIE & RYAN. I never felt someone's emotions so strongly before.

(Pause.)

KATIE. I called an Uber.

RYAN. I showed her the door.

KATIE. Should've asked for his number.

RYAN. Wanted to ask to see her again.

KATIE & RYAN. But I didn't.

(Pause.)

RYAN. Life went on.

KATIE. I lived through my divorce.

RYAN. Back to the clubs, the bars.

KATIE. Started seeing someone. Still together, actually.

RYAN. Back to my regular.

KATIE. He's a good man.

RYAN. Lots of sex.

KATIE. And the sex is good.

RYAN. And the sex is good.

KATIE. I'm more open now.

RYAN. Women come and go.

KATIE. Sexually speaking.

RYAN. It is what it is.
KATIE. Things turned out better than expected.
RYAN. Can't complain about anything.
KATIE & RYAN. But that night.

(Pause.)

RYAN. I can't get it –
KATIE. – out of my mind –
RYAN. – and it's not the sex –
KATIE. – I think about –
KATIE & RYAN. It's the moment after.

(Pause.)

KATIE. His face.
RYAN. Her face.
KATIE. Etched on my mind.
RYAN. Always with me.

(Pause.)

KATIE. I think I used him.
RYAN. I think I love her.

Pining

Banna Desta

PINING was first produced by Theater Masters in Aspen, Colorado from February 11–13, 2018. The performance was directed by Joseph Ward, and the production stage manager was Mark C. Hoffner. The cast was as follows:

SHANDUKANI................................... Christina Cappelli

PINING was first produced by Theater Masters and Rattlestick Playwrights Theater in New York City from May 1–5, 2018. The performance was directed by Joseph Ward, and the production stage manager was Deidre Works. The cast was as follows:

SHANDUKANI..................................... Ngozi Anyanwu

CHARACTERS

One actor plays **SHANDUKANI** and provides voices for the following:
SHANDU'S DAD
CHILDHOOD FRIEND
LIAM
HELEN
KOFI

(SHANDUKANI enters the center of the stage.)

SHANDUKANI. I have a crush, and most days it feels like a personal attack on my life. There's nothing profound about that or even interesting. It just is.

My creepy habits come to the fore when I'm crushing. I notice even the smallest details like what shoes they wear regularly, what they eat at lunch or when they seem sleepy.

Liam's my crush. He's goofy and admittedly kind of *strange* looking. I'm talking lanky, beak nose with chicken legs strange. Liam's from Munster, Ireland. Hadn't heard of it either, but whenever he opens his mouth, everyone swoons because Americans are fetishy weirdos who swoon when they hear a Euro accent. I won't lie I swooned too. At first. Then I remembered all the times people mocked my African parents growing up.

(Actor speaks with South African accent for **SHANDU'S DAD***'s lines.)*

SHANDU'S DAD. "Eh, Shandu! Go on and blow out de berfday cando."

CHILDHOOD FRIEND. *(Whispers.)* "Why does your dad talk like that?"

SHANDU'S DAD. "Come, come Shandu-eh."

SHANDUKANI. "I don't know. It's just how he talks."

CHILDHOOD FRIEND. "It's kind of weird."

(Beat.)

SHANDUKANI. I should have slapped that bitch. Can someone please tell me what makes a South Irish accent more enchanting than a South African one?

Anyway, I forgot to mention, Liam's white. Like, pasty white. And sometimes, when he's nervous, he turns pink and red. He sits in the cubicle in front of me, so I can always see the tip top of his light, brown hair.

I knew I liked him when he wanted to know how to pronounce my name.

*(Actor speaks with an Irish accent when reciting **LIAM**'s lines.)*

LIAM. "Shand– Shanduk– Shandukanny?"

SHANDUKANI. "Shandukani."

LIAM. "Ah, I'm a fuckin' arse, I'll get it right I promise."

SHANDUKANI. "That's okay, everyone just calls me Shandu"

LIAM. "No, I'm determined. People ought to say your name the proper way. Least they can do."

SHANDUKANI. Liam is *kind* with a sense of humor that makes even the coldest heart thaw.

But apparently, I'm not the only one who was smitten. Every day there'd be a new person hunched over the front of his cubicle, flirting. Sarah, the copywriter. Alice the editor. Bruce the maintenance guy?

Naturally, I did the only thing one can do when afraid of unrequited affection – I became a real bitch to him.

A couple days ago, he turned around to ask me for a favor.

LIAM. "Hey Shandukani, could I borrow your badge to take the lift to the ninth floor?"

SHANDUKANI. "We don't call it *lift* in America, it's the elevator, but sure."

LIAM. "Sorry, mate."

SHANDUKANI. I felt bad of course, but wanted to make sure there was no trace that I'm actually pressed. But wait, did he just call me mate? We're not JUST friends.

LIAM. "I like what you've done with your hair, Shandu!"

SHANDUKANI. "Thanks."

LIAM. "What kind of style is that?"

SHANDUKANI. "They're box braids."

LIAM. "Lovely."

SHANDUKANI. Don't ask me about my hair. I don't care if I'm infatuated with you or not. Yeah, I love it *now*, but it's a sore subject for *other* reasons.

(Beat.)

Often, I'll wonder if Liam is "into" black girls and I hate myself for thinking it. What I should be asking myself is if I'm into white guys. The answer is usually no.

Some days I think my boss, Helen, is on to my charade, but she'd never call me out. I think I have a crush on her too so ideally, she'd be a bit jealous.

Oh, I'm not into girls, she just happens to be a real babe. I mean we work at the most shit newspaper, oh yeah, I work at a shit newspaper, yet she still manages to churn out journalistic gold. Like Christiane Amanpour meets Joan Didion. She's too good for this place.

When I say she's a babe I mean she's the kind of woman who's as well-versed in Nietzsche as she is in *Real Housewives*.

Now, she's someone I don't mind openly pining for. I practically flirt with her. I *want* her to like me.

HELEN. "Love what you've done with your hair, Shandu!"

SHANDUKANI. "Aw, thanks Helen!"

Okay, SHE can ask me about my hair.

HELEN. "What do you call that style?"

SHANDUKANI. "They're box braids! Nothing too special, ya know."

HELEN. "LOVE IT."

SHANDUKANI. Helen is sort of racially ambiguous. I've tried to think of inventive ways to ask her where she's *from-from*, and I fear that she'll be Sicilian or Greek or something *else*. I'm selfish and I want to claim her.

Today she drove me home from work. Her car smells like fresh linens and she drives a hybrid. She's the globally responsible type. God, don't you love her too?

HELEN. "Ugh, sorry you had to sit through that meeting with Marty. I almost fell asleep three or four times."

SHANDUKANI. She's gossiping with me. You can tell someone trusts you when they gossip with you.

"Ugh, I know. No worries though, you handled it like a boss!"

HELEN. "You think? Sometimes he just rambles for so long, I lose my train of thought."

SHANDUKANI. "No, trust me. You do a great job at shutting him up."

She laughed. She thinks I'm funny.

HELEN. "Is this you?"

SHANDUKANI. She pulls up to my apartment building and for a second I wonder if I should invite her up for ice cream or something. I think she might even say yes. Then I catch her eyes wandering around, observing my neighborhood, gathering data about who I might be.

"Yup, this is me! Thanks again. I'll see you tomorrow!"

HELEN. "No problem! Get home safe!"

SHANDUKANI. She drove off, with haste. Ugh, that hurt. She thinks I'm not safe.

(Beat.)

I don't live in the hood, but I live hood-adjacent. Meaning, I live next to a housing project, but across the street from an artisanal grilled cheese shop.

I live in a quaint-*ish* one-bedroom that I can just barely afford, but I value unaccompanied nudity and sulking alone to King Krule too much to have a roommate. I mean, I have a stable-*ish* job at the paper, but I barely make ends meet. How do all the poor people around me do it? How did my parents do it?

(Ponders.)

Different story for a different play.

I walk up to my apartment and bump into Kofi at the mailbox.

Kofi is hot and I will happily objectify him.

He's lived in the apartment across from mine for years, and it remains the biggest mystery to me. I mean, I've never really seen him leave the house to go to work and he's always wearing a wife-beater. His muscles protrude and I want so badly to run my fingers over every bulging vein.

I think I know what he does for a living, but I don't want to know too much. He's not paying my bills and I enjoy looking at him so much that ignorance is bliss.

KOFI. "Shandu, how you doin' baby sis?"

SHANDUKANI. Oh yeah, I forgot to tell you he calls me "sis."

"Ahhh, I'm good Kofi. What you been up to, it's been a minute."

KOFI. "You know what it is, same old, same old. Get the mail, get a fresh cut. I seen your name in the paper and told everybody in the barbershop, THAT'S MY NEIGHBOR."

SHANDUKANI. I want to climb him.

"HAHAHA, you know it's nothing, real local stuff."

KOFI. "Nah, nah, you smart, Shandu. That's why I fuck with you."

SHANDUKANI. I want *you* to fuck *me*, Kofi.

"Aww thanks big bro! You're too kind."

We walk up two flights together and he smells so potently of cocoa butter, it inspires me to bake a chocolate cake tonight. I fiddle with my keys, watching him unlock his door before he walks in. He turns to me and we lock eyes...for just a moment. A pure moment.

KOFI. "Okay, Shandu, you gon' have to send me the links to some of them articles you're so good at writing."

SHANDUKANI. "Aww, you really don't have to read them."

KOFI. "I gotta support the sisters."

SHANDUKANI. I fake laugh with him, and look into his apartment, locking eyes with the chick on the couch for a second before he walks in and closes the door behind him.

I've seen types like her in his apartment PLENTY of times before. Kofi's house is the United Nations of non-black POC women. I'm talking Korean, Chinese,

Indian, Cambodia, Thai, white-passing Colombians, Puerto Ricans, Brazilians, the list is endless. They're always in and out.

Ugh, but *we* could be so good together and he just doesn't know it. But, Kofi is a drug dealer and I'm an average journalist. Our worlds are too different and I am his *"little sister."*

Sometimes I wonder what would happen if I told Liam I wanted him. Or if I told Helen I want to be sisters. Or even if I told Kofi I *desperately* want to fuck him.

What's the worst that could happen, anyway? Alright, here it goes. I'll write them emails!

> (**SHANDUKANI** *pretends to stand at a desk, making typing motions while reading her emails.*)

"Dear Liam, I know you think I hate you, but the truth is I'd like to delicately make out with you to Crime Mob playing lightly in the background. Sorry for all the badgering at work. Let's link over a beer soon?"

Then Helen.

"Dear Helen, WE NEED TO BE BEST FRIENDS. We could stay up and have Nora Ephron marathons. I really wouldn't mind being the Gayle to your Oprah. Sounds fun, right? Let me know when you're free."

And last but not least, Kofi.

"Dear Kofi, I want to change your life, sexually and intellectually. Fuck me. *PLEASE. PLEASE PLEASE.* See you at home."

> (*Beat.*)

Did I have you there for a second? I'm not *that* crazy. Or I guess, I am. Just no one knows it.

Yeah, I'd like to just say how I feel, but I can't show my cards unless I know precisely how they feel about me. And I worry that *not* saying it out loud means I'll never change. Is that so bad? Is that selfish? Yeah, yeah, I'm the silently tortured type.

I wonder about who I will eventually desire next. After all, we're all quietly pining for *someone*. Will it be the mailman? A mutual friend? A stranger at the gym? Just kidding, I don't go to the gym.

I have a crush, or I guess you could say crushes, and most days it feels like a personal attack on my life. There's nothing profound about that or even interesting. It just is.

   (Blackout.)

Slap

Aja Nisenson

SLAP was first produced by Theater Masters in Aspen, Colorado from February 11–13, 2018. The performance was directed by Joanie Schultz, and the production stage manager was Mark C. Hoffner. The cast was as follows:

MOM...Eileen Seeley
DAUGHTER ....Izzi Rojo
DAD... Franz C. Alderfer

SLAP was first produced by Theater Masters and Rattlestick Playwrights Theater in New York City from May 1–5, 2018. The performance was directed by Joanie Schultz, and the production stage manager was Deidre Works. The cast was as follows:

MOM..Kathryn Kates
DAUGHTER ....Lilli Stein
DAD..Jim Shankman

CHARACTERS

MOM – (mid-sixties) A knock-out in her youth. She wears turtlenecks (like Diane Keaton) to hide what has become of her neck with age.

DAUGHTER – (mid-twenties) A tick riding the hair of a deer.

DAD – (late fifties) A Brooklyn lager. Would walk around in his boxers all day if he could.

SETTING

The kitchen of a suburban household in New Jersey.

TIME

Thanksgiving, present.

*(The kitchen. **MOM** stands facing her **DAUGHTER**. One side of **MOM**'s face is completely swollen. They are mid-argument.)*

DAUGHTER. Forget it.

MOM. Why not?

DAUGHTER. Because I'm not.

MOM. I don't see what the big deal is.

DAUGHTER. Mom, I'm not slapping or punching you in the face, so forget it.

MOM. Well I'm not going to Thanksgiving dinner with one side of my face all swollen like a chipmunk. Either you punch me on the other side and my whole entire face is swollen or I'm not going at all. Look at me!

DAUGHTER. I don't understand why you picked the worst possible time to get Botox.

MOM. It's dermal filler, and she said I'd be swollen for a week max. Not two weeks!

DAUGHTER. Can't you cover it up with makeup? That seems like a much less painful solution.

MOM. I tried that. Nothing works.

DAUGHTER. What about Dad? I'm sure he wants to punch you. Can't you get Dad to do this?

MOM. No. Your father's impossible. You know what he's like. It's like being married to a golden retriever except not as obedient and hairier.

*(**DAD** enters in his boxers.)*

DAD. I'm not here.

MOM. He never listens to me except when I don't want him to.

DAD. I heard that.

MOM. *(To **DAUGHTER**.)* See?

(**DAD** *goes to the fridge and drinks out of the milk carton.*)

DAD. Has anyone seen my wallet? Or my cell phone?

MOM. Where's the last place you had it?

DAD. *(Joking.)* The strip club.

MOM. Very funny. Your father thinks he's a comedian.
(*To* **DAUGHTER.**) He can't keep track of anything. He literally has two things to keep track of and he can never find them. Every other second it's: "Where's my wallet? Have you seen my cell phone?"

DAD. Call my flip phone, will you?

DAUGHTER. You still have a flip phone?! They're like vintage. You could sell it on eBay and probably get a lot of money for it. Some hipster would probably buy it. Mom, where's your phone? Dad, do you really want me to call it?

MOM. In my bag.

DAUGHTER. Where's your bag?

MOM. Check the freezer.

DAUGHTER. The freezer?

MOM. Your father was cleaning up. I didn't know where else to put it. He throws out all my things.

(**DAUGHTER** *goes to the freezer to get Mom's bag.*)

DAD. *(To* **MOM.**) You haven't seen my wallet have you?

MOM. I swear to god if I have to hear one more time about your wallet I'm going to scream. Did you check the car? Or the bathroom? You're always leaving everything in the bathroom.

(**DAUGHTER** *pulls out Mom's cell phone.*)

DAUGHTER. I don't see Dad's name in your contacts.

MOM. It's under "Nincompoop."

DAUGHTER. You're joking, right?

MOM. No. It's after "Kvetch" and before "Schmuck."

(To **DAD**.*)* Can you please look in the car Eric? Because if it's not in there I'm going to have to call the police again to file a report.

> (**DAUGHTER** *calls Dad's cell phone. An old flip phone ringtone is heard in the distance.** **DAD** *exits.*)

DAD. *(Answering the phone.)* Hello?

> (**DAUGHTER** *puts Mom's bag on the table.*)
>
> *(A beat.)*
>
> (**MOM** *sees her* **DAUGHTER** *for the first time. That is, she sees what she is wearing.*)

DAUGHTER. What?

> *(A beat.)*

MOM. Are you wearing that?

DAUGHTER. What's wrong with this?

> (**MOM** *rummages through/organizes her pocketbook throughout the following dialogue. Her bag is like Mary Poppins'.* **MOM** *pulls out everything imaginable, including but not limited to: checkbook, pens, five pairs of reading glasses,* New Yorker *magazine, floss, plastic fork, hard candies, Tums, deodorant, makeup, stamps, tissues, jewelry, one glove, winter hat, tennis ball, snow globe, etc.*)

MOM. Nothing honey. It's just you look so good in red. You're always wearing black. When you get to be my age you can wear black. What about some lipstick?

DAUGHTER. For whom? The turkey? Am I trying to look good for the turkey?

MOM. For you. You'll feel better if you put on some lipstick. It wouldn't hurt you to put on some lipstick.

---

*A license to produce *Theater Masters' Take Ten, Vol. IV* does not include a performance license for any third-party or copyrighted music. Licensees should create an original composition or use music in the public domain. For further information, please see Music Use Note on page 3.

DAUGHTER. I'm not putting on some lipstick.

MOM. Fine.

(A beat.)

What about your hair?

DAUGHTER. You know what? Maybe I *should* punch you in the face.

MOM. You're beautiful sweetheart. You know I think you're breathtakingly beautiful. I just want the rest of the world to see it.

DAD. *(Calling to* **MOM.***)* Have you seen my wallet?!

MOM. *(Calling to* **DAD.***)* Did you leave it in the car?!

DAD. *(Calling to* **MOM.***)* I don't think so!

MOM. *(Calling to* **DAD.***)* Did you look?!!

DAUGHTER. Why is everyone yelling?

MOM. We're not yelling. This is how we talk.

*(**MOM** pulls out a can opener from her bag.)*

DAUGHTER. Is that a can opener?

*(**MOM** pulls out a can of tuna fish from her bag.)*

MOM. Tuna fish. I like to carry around a little protein.

DAUGHTER. You can't carry around some nuts like a normal person?

MOM. You're shaving your legs aren't you honey? Because I read this article in the paper about single women in New York not shaving their legs.

(A beat).

What's that look?

DAUGHTER. Nothing.

MOM. You could wear a paper bag and still look beautiful.

DAUGHTER. Good, because this is what I'm wearing tonight.

MOM. What about some eyeliner? Because right now I just... I just don't know where to look. My eyes just keeps circling.

DAUGHTER. Your eyes just keeps circling? Did you really just say that?

MOM. Oh, you know what I mean.

DAUGHTER. No, I don't know what you mean. Your eyes just keep circling? What does that even mean? That is possibly the meanest thing anyone's ever said to me.

MOM. Oh stop it. I didn't mean it like that. I meant you have such beautiful eyes why not accentuate them.

DAUGHTER. That's not what you said.

MOM. That's what I meant.

DAUGHTER. Maybe I shouldn't go to Thanksgiving dinner. Can you punch *me* in the face so *I* can't go?

    (**MOM** *slaps her.*)

What the fuck?! Did you really just slap me?

MOM. I lightly tapped you.

DAUGHTER. What is wrong with you?

MOM. It wasn't a *slap*. It was a *tap*. I lightly *tapped* you. It didn't even leave a mark.

DAUGHTER. You're unbelievable.

MOM. Tap me. Go ahead. I tapped you, now you tap me.

DAUGHTER. I am a non-violent person. I practice ahimsa. Non-violent action.

MOM. This isn't violent. This is cosmetic. You are so selfish. Do you know how many daughters would pay good money to punch their mothers in the face? You were always a difficult child. Everyone else loved gymnastics. Everyone else was excited to go to kindergarten. You were the only one who refused to get your hearing tested in preschool. You refused the hearing test! I mean no kid did that but you. From the time you were born you had a real attitude.

DAUGHTER. From the time I was born? How is that possible? At three weeks I was giving you attitude?

MOM. Yes.

DAUGHTER. Isn't *attitude* reserved for teenagers? What exactly was I doing at three weeks? Was I talking back? I couldn't even talk. Was I giving you the finger? I couldn't even lift my finger. I didn't even know what my middle finger was! And maybe if I had a normal name I wouldn't have been so difficult.

MOM. What's wrong with Brontë *["Brontay"]*?

DAUGHTER. Nothing if you're in nineteenth-century England.

MOM. I give up! I can never do anything right everything I do is wrong nothing I say is right I can't say anything right.

DAUGHTER. Stop saying mean things.

MOM. What have I said that's mean?

DAUGHTER. Never mind.

MOM. I'm sorry you're so sensitive to everything I say.

DAUGHTER. Is that supposed to be an apology?

MOM. I can't even apologize correctly.

(**DAD** *enters.*)

DAD. Has anyone seen my pants?

DAUGHTER. Dad, why doesn't Mom just love me for who I am?

MOM. I do *too* love you for who you are.

DAUGHTER. Then stop trying to change me!

DAD. *(To* **DAUGHTER.***)* You can't take your mother seriously. I never have. That's the secret of our marriage.

MOM. *(To* **DAD.***)* What is that supposed to mean?

DAD. When you tell me you want a divorce. It doesn't *actually* mean you want a divorce.

MOM. Yes it does!

DAD. *(To* **DAUGHTER.***)* Your mother says things she doesn't mean.

MOM. Your father doesn't listen to anything I say. Nothing I say matters to your father.

DAD. I'm listening. Go ahead. Say something. I'll summarize it.

MOM. *(To* **DAUGHTER.***)* I have never felt loved by you.

DAUGHTER. You should be saying this to Dad, not me.

MOM. This isn't about your father. Your father already knows I don't feel loved by him. That's nothing new.

DAD. *(To* **DAUGHTER.***)* Everything you say she takes as a criticism. You just look at her funny and she thinks you're criticizing.

(To **MOM.***)* It's because your mother was so critical you're so sensitive to it.

MOM. This is not about my mother! This is about my daughter not loving me.

DAD. I'm kidding.

MOM. You're not kidding. Your father says "just kidding," but he's not kidding. It's passive-aggressive.

DAD. Oh stop analyzing me.

MOM. It's the truth.

DAD. *(À la Jack Nicholson.)* "You can't handle the truth."

(A beat.)

Is that tuna?

*(***DAD*** grabs the can of tuna and exits.)*

MOM. Everyone I run into keeps on telling me I look tired. You know what it's like to constantly be told you look tired?

DAUGHTER. Are you tired?

MOM. No! People say you look tired when they actually mean you need plastic surgery.

DAUGHTER. Who cares what anybody else thinks.

MOM. I envy you. It must be liberating to not give a shit how you look.

(A beat.)

I meant that as a compliment.

DAUGHTER. I didn't ask to be born, Mom.

MOM. I didn't ask for a daughter like you. I wanted you to be a plastic surgeon. You know, my friend Harriet's really lucky, her daughter punched her *and* she's a plastic surgeon.

DAUGHTER. I am not going to be manipulated. I am a grown woman. My mother is not going to get to me.
(Chanting her mantra.) I am a grown woman. My mother is not going to get to me. I am a grown woman. My mother is not going to get to me. I am a grown woman. My mother is not going to get to me.

MOM. What are you doing?

DAUGHTER. I am a grown woman. My mother is not going to get to me. I am a grown woman. My mother is not going to get to me.

DAUGHTER.	**MOM.**
I am a grown woman. My mother is not going to get to me. I am a grown woman. My mother is not going to get to me...	Who was the one who fed you and bathed you and slept with your physics professor so you'd get an "A"?

DAUGHTER. What?!

MOM. I did!

DAUGHTER.	**MOM.**
My mother is not going to get to me. I am a grown woman. My mother is not going to get to me. I am a grown woman. My mother is not going to get to me. I am a grown woman. My mother is not going to get to me. I am a grown woman. My mother is not going to get to me. I am a grown woman. My mother is not going to get to me. I am a grown woman. My mother is not going to get to me –	I was the one who mopped the vomit off your duvet when you were eight because you'd eaten too much Charleston Chew. Because that's what mothers do. I've never asked anything of you in your entire life. The least you can do is punch me. Punch me!!! Punch me you disgusting stupid incompetent imbecile! This is why you're never going to amount to anything! This is why you're single and lonely and ugly and unloveable and pathetic and lazy and –

*(**DAUGHTER** slaps **MOM** across the face. The slap is out of her control – a result of provocation, caveman instinct, and unresolved anger she was never able to express as a child.)*

*(**MOM** slaps **DAUGHTER**. **DAUGHTER** gasps.)*

*(**DAUGHTER** slaps **MOM**. **MOM** gasps.)*

(There is some cathartic release in the slaps. As if each slap brings them closer together. Their slaps hold centuries of mother/daughter strife.)

MOM. Come on, you can do better than that.

*(**DAUGHTER** punches **MOM** in the face. **MOM** falls down.)*

DAUGHTER. Mom?! ...Mom?

*(**DAUGHTER** looks up, unsure of what she just did.)*

T3MP0RARY

Joe Samaniego

T3MPORARY was first produced by Theater Masters in Aspen, Colorado from February 11–13, 2018. The performance was directed by Wes Grantom, and the production stage manager was Mark C. Hoffner. The cast was as follows:

VERONICA	Taylor Hartsfield
SERVER BOT	Shelly Marolt
VERA	Beth Caudill
JUSTIN	Joeli Villa
CAROLINE	Ciara Morrison
UNCLE ROY	Willie Mossley

T3MPORARY was first produced by Theater Masters and Rattlestick Playwrights Theater in New York City from May 1–5, 2018. The performance was directed by Wes Grantom, and the production stage manager was Deidre Works. The cast was as follows:

VERONICA	Mikaela Izquierdo
SERVER BOT	Eli Tokash
VERA	Lilli Stein
JUSTIN	Grant Harrison
CAROLINE	Alea Shae Niziak
UNCLE ROY	Jim Shankman

CHARACTERS

VERONICA – the voice of a girl in her twenties
SERVER BOT – the voice of the server's moderator
VERA – Veronica's childhood best friend who was eventually forgotten about
JUSTIN – Veronica's ex-boyfriend
CAROLINE – a girl who died at Veronica's high school
UNCLE ROY – Veronica's morally loose uncle with staunch right-wing political views

SETTING

Temporary storage

TIME

Modern day – Infinite

(Stage in darkness. The tapping sound of a keyboard/phone.)

VERONICA. Scary accident, but I'm doing well. Recovering slowly. Really puts life into perspective. Hashtag Blessed to have so many people who care about me.

> *(Bright flashing lights and static sounds. **VERA** appears in a spotlight, posing as if for a profile picture. A moment, then she becomes animated. Random lights blink in the darkness.)*

VERA. What the hell was that? Hello? Hello?

SERVER BOT. Service. Time out. Locating – Locating – Locating –

JUSTIN. Jesus, how many times are you going to say it?

> *(**JUSTIN** storms into the pool of light.)*

VERA. Justin?!

JUSTIN. Vera? Is that –

VERA. What's –

JUSTIN. – Going on? Where do I start –

> *(**VERA** looks down at herself.)*

VERA. Why do I look fifteen? And you – you haven't –

JUSTIN. Here, you should sit down.

VERA. Oh, god. I have Kool-Aid in my hair. Why did I ever do that?

JUSTIN. This is going to sound weird but...you look this way because your profile picture looks this way. This, you, all of it, is your profile.

VERA. I'm a profile? But, I'm me. I feel like –

JUSTIN. You are you, technically, a profile of you, but... You've been deleted.

VERA. Deleted?! From where?

JUSTIN. Veronica... She deleted you.

SERVER BOT. System. Boot. Scanning. Scanning.

>   (**VERA** *looks up.*)

JUSTIN. It's the server wiping unnecessary data, you get used to it.

VERA. Why would Veronica delete me? This is some sort of mistake.

JUSTIN. Veronica tends to forget about people. You're not the only one, she deleted me too.

VERA. She had a reason to delete you, not me.

JUSTIN. You guys haven't talked in years. Why would she keep you?

VERA. Oh shut up, Justin, you cheated on her in Havasu.

JUSTIN. But I told her about it!

VERA. So?

JUSTIN. I could have kept it a secret.

VERONICA. Best husband in the world – /

VERA. / Hey! Hello?!

VERONICA. Look at the flowers he brought me! Hashtag Blessed. Heart emoji. Heart emoji.

VERA. Was that Veronica?

JUSTIN. Mhm... She's posting. We're stuck in her news feed.

SERVER BOT. Uploading... Uploading... Post Successful.

>   (*A bright light from above.* **JUSTIN** *and* **VERA** *look up.*)

JUSTIN. She looks...happy.

VERA. Veronica, it's me! Vera? Remember?

JUSTIN. It's no use, it's just a picture. She can't hear you.

VERA. What is this place?

JUSTIN. I guess... Where all the things Veronica forgets about go.

>   (*The sound of a slow-clap comes from the darkness.* **UNCLE ROY** *enters. He looks*

> *like that guy in the background of every family Thanksgiving picture. Wine, glasses, mustache, red sweater, belly, and sweat.)*

UNCLE ROY. You finally learned the truth. My niece is a ruthless snowflake!

JUSTIN. Leave her alone, Roy. She just got here.

UNCLE ROY. We all know she deleted me because she couldn't handle the truth! She didn't want to believe me that Trump was gunna win and that he was gunna be good for this country. Goddamned fake news gets it wrong I tell ya – Heads stuck in sand! Ostrich people!

JUSTIN. I won't be baited into another political argument with you. Remember our deal? Back to your side!

UNCLE ROY. Fine! I'm going to take a nap. When I get back we'll talk about North Korea and the Second Amendment. Now those are two things we can all agree on.

> (**UNCLE ROY** *vanishes into the darkness.*)

JUSTIN. Really makes you think though. If I'm lumped in with *that* guy it's gotta be a mistake, right?

VERA. It has to be. Hello! Hey! There seems to be a mistake. Uh – Error. I think you – or somebody deleted me – My name is Vera – Vera Johnson! Command, backslash, process.

SERVER BOT. Processing.

JUSTIN. Hello?! Hey!

SERVER BOT. Processing.

JUSTIN. It's never said that before.

VERA. Maybe it knows it made a mistake? If it put us here, it can put us back right?

> *(Beat.)*

Um, backslash, reboot, uh –

JUSTIN. Hey, um. So, my name is Justin Chatsworth. Justin –

SERVER BOT. 500 Internal Service Error.

JUSTIN. Chatsworth!

SERVER BOT. System, scanning. System. Error. Error.

JUSTIN. Maybe we should be careful messing with the system.

VERA. We're not completely erased, which means...we are in a network, a storage, of sorts, right? Which means, there has to be an exit or a source file.

JUSTIN. I haven't found any sort of exit. What are you –

VERA. The system is actively scanning data, if we can get to the recycling bin –

(VERA moves in and out of light she tries to head off.)

JUSTIN. I already tried that... All I found were old pictures of us, emails from her dad and her old email address: socalcutiexo27@yahoo.com.

VERA. Maybe she will see my file in there and realize –

JUSTIN. Why are you so hung up on this? You're just another thing Veronica forgot about.

VERA. I was deleted! People just don't – delete each other – just like that and I – We were best friends and I loved her –

VERONICA. Today I think back on my life. The late nights. The sunrises. The scraped knees and the fear. I remember it now like it was an endless, towering experience. And I feel so happy to have shared that with all of you. The people who matter. Teethsmileemoji.

(Pause.)

VERA. We mattered to her, didn't we? Justin?

JUSTIN. I tried to tell you... Her life keeps moving on and we're stuck here. She's some place totally different.

VERA. I knew we grew distant but... I didn't think she would forget me, just like that. About all of it.

JUSTIN. I thought the same thing... But one day I found a file full of terrible things she meant to send to people – her family – me – you – her husband – spanning years and years, byte after byte...

VERA. About me? What did I ever do to –

JUSTIN. Let's just say you learn a lot about somebody when you see their temporary thoughts. She may have never sent them, but she meant them.

VERA. We can make her remember. System. Backslash. Compose.

SERVER BOT. Invalid request. Corrupted source.

UNCLE ROY. *(Offstage.)* I forgot to tell you! United Airlines is scamming us out of our money!

(The light flickers. Computer noises.)

SERVER BOT. Error. Error. System –

JUSTIN. What did you do to the system?

VERA. If we can compose a file, a virus, something we can give her a message, we can make her remember. We can make her – System. Command. Execute.

(Pools of light flicker on and off throughout the stage violently. Finally, the light stops and **CAROLINE** *has "entered.")*

CAROLINE. Finally, people!

JUSTIN & VERA. Whoa shit! / Jesus!

VERA. Caroline? Caroline Fowler? I thought – you were...

CAROLINE. I'm...what?

VERA. Nine years ago you – died...

CAROLINE. My profile still exists I guess.

(The lights flicker again.)

SERVER BOT. 500 Internal Service Error.

CAROLINE. I'm glad I found you when I did. In the other sectors profiles have been disappearing, data has been lost and –

JUSTIN. Where did you come from?

CAROLINE. In the downloads folder there were noises and – these things erasing the sky. All words, pictures, vanished.

VERA. How far away was that?

CAROLINE. I can't tell. The files have gotten smaller. I think the system is collapsing.

(**UNCLE ROY** *enters.*)

UNCLE ROY. I mean, when it comes down to abortion, let's get real people –

(*Lights go dark. Lights back up.* **UNCLE ROY** *has vanished.*)

JUSTIN. Did the system just purge Roy?

CAROLINE. This is what was happening where I was. People, profiles would just vaporize!

VERA. Whoa! Okay! Hey, system! This was a mistake I didn't mean to – I'm not!

JUSTIN. Hey! Yeah! Me too!

VERA. Caroline. When those things erased the sky could you see out of the system? Could you see anything?

CAROLINE. No. It was nothing. It wasn't white or clear. God, I can't explain it to you.

SERVER BOT. 0010011101010.

JUSTIN. Okay. Here's what we do. We sit here and we wait it out, okay? It's probably dumping unnecessary data and – we'll be fine as long as we stay here.

VERA. Do you see the erasers?

CAROLINE. ...No.

JUSTIN. Then it will pass. It will...

CAROLINE. I don't want to be erased, if this is it – If this is all I can be –

VERA. It's going to be fine. We're going to be fine.

CAROLINE. I want you to know – I wasn't – When I died it wasn't miraculous it was – I was trying to explain I was – There was –

(**CAROLINE** *vanishes.*)

JUSTIN. Fuck! Where did she go?

VERA. Justin?! Is it going to erase us?

VERONICA. It – Have – Beautiful Vacation – Pal – Palm – Error – I – And I – And I – And I – And I – And I – And I – And I – And I –

(Grating electronic noises. Lights flicker then lights at full. Stark-white emptiness.)

VERA. What just –

JUSTIN. Did it just wipe out?

VERA. Are we still?

JUSTIN. I think...

*(**JUSTIN** and **VERA** walk around the space.)*

VERA. Holy shit I thought for sure that was the end!

JUSTIN. It must've passed over us? But... Why?

VERA. I don't know... Maybe the system knows we were put here by mistake? Or maybe Veronica noticed us after all?

JUSTIN. You were right.

VERA. I guess so...

JUSTIN. I didn't want to believe she deleted me...

(Beat.)

You know Vera, it might make you feel better. When I was looking through her files I did find something she wrote about you – It seemed genuinely –

*(**JUSTIN** vanishes.)*

VERA. Justin?! Hey! Hello?!

*(**VERA** in emptiness. No sound.)*

VERONICA. Sometimes in life – Sometimes – Life in – In sometimes – Life – In – In – In – Life – Sometime in Life – We forget. And that's okay and that's okay and –

VERA. Veronica, you have to hear me, please, listen to me – Please –

VERONICA. We forget and – And we forget and – It's okay –

SERVER BOT. Error. Error. Error.

VERA. You said that already! Control Alt Delete! Veronica! Somebody! Backslash. Command. Draft message.

SERVER BOT. *(Repeated. Fading out.)* Information Error – 404 Not Found.

> *(Over the following speech, growing beeps and computer noises dominate the space. Something about this seems dissonant and disfigured.* **VERA** *is fighting against the end.)*

VERA. This is how you remember me? This is who I am? And this is where I stay? And this is how I'm forgotten and this – And I want you to know – If – When I'm forgotten – and it goes away. And I – I remember those scraped knees. And I feel afraid – But when I remember – And when I think about that time – when it fell apart – I forget – And I'm sorry – I wanted to be there – I want to be there – And I just wanted to say to you –

> *(An ugly, technological noise. Abrupt blackout. Silence.)*

End of Play

www.ingramcontent.com/pod-product-compliance
Lightning Source LLC
Chambersburg PA
CBHW051409290426
44108CB00015B/2220